Nothing Fell Today But Rain

15 November 2008

Nothing Fell Today But Rain

Poems by
~~Evan Jones~~

For Todd, on the occasion of our meeting in London.

E. Jones

Fitzhenry & Whiteside

Nothing Fell Today But Rain
Copyright © 2003 Fitzhenry & Whiteside

All rights reserved. No part of this book may be reproduced in any manner without the express written consent of the publisher, except in the case of brief excerpts in critical reviews and articles. All inquiries should be addressed to:

Fitzhenry & Whiteside Limited
195 Allstate Parkway
Markham, Ontario L3R 4T8

In the United States:
121 Harvard Avenue, Suite 2
Allston, Massachusetts 02134

www.fitzhenry.ca   godwit@fitzhenry.ca

Fitzhenry & Whiteside acknowledges with thanks the Canada Council for the Arts, the Government of Canada through its Book Publishing Industry Development Program, and the Ontario Arts Council for their support of our publishing program.

National Library of Canada Cataloguing in Publication Data

Jones, Evan, 1973-
        Nothing fell today but rain / Evan Jones.
Poems.
ISBN 1-55041-750-9
    I. Title.
PS8569.O517N58 2003   C811'.6   C2003-900589-5
PR9199.4.J65N58 2003

U.S. Publisher Cataloging-in-Publication Data

Jones, Evan.
  Nothing fell today but rain / Evan Jones.-- 1st ed.
[96] p. : cm.
Summary: Contemporary poetry
ISBN 1-55041-750-9 (pbk.)
1. Canadian poetry -- 21st century. I. Title.
811.54 21   PR9195.72   .J762.N91   2003

Cover/book design by: Karen Petherick, Intuitive Design International Ltd.,
                           Peterborough, Ontario
Cover art: Jean Dallaire, *Le Pont/The Bridge*, 1965, Oil on canvas.
                         Copyright © Estate of Jean Dallaire/SODRAC (Montreal) 2003.
Printed and bound in Canada.

For Teeana and Tré

Children, O armour against sleep, look,
even the sun rises in mourning
beneath your weariness.

Contents

1. Oneiropoems 9
2. On Cowardice 31
3. The Spine of Cities 47
4. Nostalgia and, Also, Anomie 57
5. A Poetics of Highways 81

Index of Titles 101

Acknowledgements 103

Oneiropoems

My friend, dreams are things hard to interpret, hopeless to puzzle
out, and people find that not all of them end in anything.
There are two pairs of gates through which the insubstantial dreams issue.
One pair of gates is made of horn, and one of ivory.
Those of the dreams which issue through the gate of sawn ivory,
these are deceptive dreams, their message is never accomplished.
But those that come into the open through the gates of polished
horn accomplish the truth for any mortal who sees them.

   The Odyssey

Meditation on a Desired Reader

I

I write to you across the absence of breath.

II

Among the books in my collection, only three refer to you directly. Αναγνώστησ. *Lecteur.*

III

To you, lovers "want to eat;" a lie is "irrelevant;" meetings are "in Paris;" books are "through;" confusion is "drawing fish;" new painters "are needed;" sleep "passes time;" a promise is "never again."

IV

You arrive hungry with the morning, a desire and another desire having filled your young breast. "There's a funny sort of comfort in your work," you stipple, "a love and another love. So many different days. I want a church wedding and some time to myself."

V

Ce que je sais
Ce qui est vrai.
Αυτά είναι τα ψέματα τον ποιητόν.

VI

Funny how the mind works. Paris, city of heartsickness and cold June rain, becomes a symptom of my poetry. Meanwhile, here in Weston, I tire of meditation; osmosis; masturbation; self-pity; candlelight; music; shadow puppets; melatonin; Spanish wine; letter-writing; reading; sleep. "Whatever of you is in there is not ephemeral." Yes, but my weak heart, my everyday.

VII

Three signs of a book mentioning readers—breathlessness—infidelity—eczema.

VIII

I can't make it in to the office today. My heartsickness is acting up. It is very kind of you to look at me and not look at me. To those unfortunates who remember Eros, you are "disciplined against desire."

IX

"This wrong toy is just the box of a chair."

X

Your soul, too, has its dust. And, you might say, my concern, both voluntary and involuntary, is really just poetry's humility. "You do not understand me." Hanging on your lips: be quiet for once. "I am not talking about your poetry."

XI

New painters, like apple or pear trees, are grown in fields. Well it's no cause for concern, I only mention it to complete the still life. The simile is lost on me, anyway.

XII

Morning and night, it's you I am thinking of. And isn't it odd that one of my books has fallen into your hands? "God, people, you know, love their work."

XIII

For every poem that begins with absence, there are three readers whispering, "Hold onto me. Hold onto me." Here is my first apology, one time I will never come back.

XIV

Like hiding a flower from the sun, I haven't been sleeping well. It may explain this awkward beauty. "You lie there and think of lines, wondering why you don't know any promises. It's easier for you, that's all. Your love of lines, lines and promises."

XV

O ma poésie aime.
Ἡ ανάσα του ποιητή.

XVI

When work is done, either you are somewhere suffering or you are somewhere not suffering. Still, I can never stay mad at you. And even if no one hears your breathing—at last a promise!—I will write to you again.

The Ivory Gate

This gate, glowing in underworld light, is for the most part redundant; the dead don't guard their secrets. It serves only as a point of departure, connecting no walls. I could tell you its height, compare its colour to that of cream or teeth, but would be teaching you nothing. Here a lover bit my cheek. I think about it every day, ignoring a telephone ringing in the other room.

The Horn Gate

It is not the sea you hear. Not one of the five rivers of Hades nor rain against the house you grew up in. Over the past four thousand years, this gate has become more popular than its partner. I wandered two weeks to get here, book in hand. On arriving, I leaned back, pressed the pages flat against my forehead, and began to cry. This is not what you hear either.

Nausicaa

She remembers only her dreaming. Refashions herself in the morning as if sleep has removed a piece of her, changed and replaced it before she woke. I, too, am at her knees, have been for some time now, but not as part of the dream. She cannot see me lying waterlogged on the sand in front of her; steps on my hand and walks by. It doesn't matter what I am. There is a certain pleasure in that.

Eros

There is no word for a person who is desired. Bear in mind how Phaedra was burnt by the sound of Hippolytus' name. This is probably for the best. In essence, her stained heart ached for love's bitterness; she had indentured herself to it. You bumped your head and let me kiss the spot you were rubbing. I awoke, desire all around me, with nothing to say.

Anteros

Imagine the breath inside you belonged to another. This may take some adjustment. Inhale. Every day, do you empty or refill your lungs? Niobe's children, their chests pierced by arrows resembling beams of morning and evening light, understood that no cherub killed them. Exhale. I worry that you might misunderstand.

Hesione

I see her by the river, hair pinned back, writing lists of possible futures for herself in the pages of a small notebook: Go to Caucasus, wait and grow old, meet someone new, etc. At night, she keeps the blinds open until midnight, hoping to see Prometheus in the street. She can't help it. More than anything she needs to know what happens next.

Lethe

This line in my open palm is a river, each ripple a memory passing into oblivion. With nowhere to ford and no bridge to cross, the other side seems distant. You held my head in your arms, face against chest, and then backed away. There I am on the southern bank, drinking handfuls of quiet water. I'm concentrating. How do my eyes look?

Mnemosyne

Eight days after constructing a building around this spring, Trophonius was struck dead, a great honour bestowed on him by Apollo. These were the memories on his lips: houses, temples, bridges. By the time I came to write this down only his spirit remained. His desire left him hidden in the fields of mourning. Even now he is planning towers, stadiums, skyscrapers.

Marsyas

He composed his first song to a new moon and, proceeding along an imagined list, continued dedicating to the sea, earth, grass, sand and finally sun. It was getting towards dawn when the telephone rang. Euterpe had left him. He wrote a song about climbing into her body. Melody. Tone. Rhythm. Mode. Skin torn from muscle. I could hear it all.

Babys

Every night since his brother died, he has repeated a mantra to himself while falling asleep. It is a list of reasons Euterpe could not love him: hands too small, can't dance, not good in bed, etc. Afterward, he dreams what he desires to dream: home, family, answering machine. All the things his brother had no use for.

Selene

In dreams of leaving Endymion, she packs dinner into a bag and is about to awaken when he finds her. "Wasn't it you who came home to an empty bed?" he oversimplifies. Beside her, when she does wake from deception, his body smells of onions and black pepper; by his shoulder on the blanket, soup stains. If they are naked, I know why the bag tore.

Evadne

For me to explain her victory is difficult: either she was waiting for the phone to ring or the ringing to stop. In any case, an answering machine wouldn't make any difference—her dreams are not messages. In one she was four-months pregnant. Another had Capaneus die on her birthday. These kinds of dreams ended her life. I imagine there was no loss involved at all.

Io

Driven by the stinging in her chest, she wakes from sleep not crying, just empty, surrounded by the sun's rising over Caucasus. Distance is her only memory. Yet she has one recurrent dream that connects to the past: my face, a telephone on fire, trying to touch her cheek. Desire urges her on without aim or sense. And then I am left burning.

Theoclymenus

I see him in Egypt, sullen, under the shelter of his father's tomb, writing descriptions of Helen's body on unbleached paper. Afraid of laying words in the grass, where bees pollinate, he instead folds the pages into swans and encloses them in eggshells. His work is not about work. Please don't ask what I mean.

Eos

"Tithonus," she called, hands trembling. The living room curtains drawn; his naked body under star light, Ethiopian cotton, a cloud of sage. Inside her dream, the little girl balances on rafters over an old man asleep. He was gone before morning. Listen. In the distance, ringing, a cicada. Thank the gods she was able to do that.

Alcyone

The difference between now and later is good night. The waves will be touching her; near her; away from her. The sun will climb higher; pass naked; sting her eyes. Now, where the Euboean Strait meets the shore of Trachis, the distance between Ceyx and her fingers is that same good night. Wait. Maybe the heat is gone. Maybe I too need rest.

Telephones in the Oneiropoems

I can say that dreams enter through sleep but, even if forgotten, dreams do not exit in the same sense. Desire, the space between my dreams and yours, travels in this way as well. The only honest statement in this book is that I have never dreamed of telephones:

1. The phone rings.
2. There is no answer.
3. The machine picks up.
4. Please get back to me.

-or-

5. Cannot come to the phone.
6. Sorry I missed your call.
7. Only just got your message.
8. Couldn't find your number.

-or-

9. Can't talk right now.
10. Will call you tomorrow.
11. There is no dial tone.
12. We have been disconnected.

-or-

13. The number is not in service.
14. Please hang up the receiver.
15. Try your call again.
16. This is a recording.

Desire grows in the space between rings; a yearning fills the void. Thank you for that. It is proof that telephones do not bridge a distance. Your voice, travelling, arrives and does not leave. It makes all the difference.

On Cowardice

...O, you, child becoming a woman, you would not deign to stoop and gather the accessible flowers and the deceptive foliage that the habitual cowardice of man tries to make into a bouquet, nothing more of your past will be able to hold you back!

—René Crevel

Till the end of their days all of them
Carried the memory of their cowardice,
For they didn't want to die without a reason.

—Czeslaw Milosz

PARDON
This morning found you lying beside me
Across the city

To live like this
Moved back into the valley where
Women tell the shore to indulge in living

I would take you anywhere
Now that sun is come round
And river banks dry whimsically in the light

To live onto you
Born when days like trees without fault
Let swallows tremble in their nests

To live across
The city like this
Pardon

TONIGHT AT LEAST, WAIT FOR ME IF YOU POSSIBLY CAN
then the sun will softly pronounce anguish in its
faltering light. Does anyone care how much this costs?
How about the eyes: We are sent recent paintings

in which to sleep, yet somehow forget that sleep
hangs from a nail in the iris, vanishing towards
the dawn of sun—moved there, captured by light.
Are you really this person, lost or worth some risk?

The mouth opens on a watercolour and pressure building
into senseless friendship. Here already I've said too much.
That was paradise, where the hands so easily penetrated
movement and would change to fit a collage we can

never go back to. The long conversations without
you, the drifting of the mind and every brief excitement
are the opposite of this. But to read the face alone
is to want you and want you to go. The canvas

hanging in anticipation thinks as much and I do know
better—not better in that what waits behind the image
of a door is only imaginable, but more like the ankles,
yours, which is all I'm left to mention these days.

The sun is setting now, and from your body the most
hurtful colours fall smiling. How much of this is
cowardice, then, with its childish urge to destroy you
or, tonight at least, to wait for you if I possibly can?

WHEN YOU WERE HUNGRY FOR BREAD I SPOKE OF BEES IN THE VALLEY
When you were thirsty for water I listed flowers
When you were tired of sleeping I still appreciated them
Isn't it nice just to talk sometimes
Water and bread and sleeping
No not sometimes
It's going out of fashion
If this only lasts three weeks it is still alright
Let's go down naked into the valley

DO YOU GROW THE NIGHT SO THAT WE GO DOWN FURTHER
    into the valley?
Do you end the middle of March and not this day so that
    sun reflects off waves in the river and a body?
Do you say such things just to hurt me?
"When in city he'll be talking as staggering vitamin."
All this has created a certain bitterness.
The mud and snow by the river around us.
The dead grass our burden.
Do you never know what grief is until sun reflects off it?
This piece of heart by the river drifting naked amid
    our burden.
Do you think it will ever believe us?

THE BRIDGE TODAY WAS CLOSED,
the bridge today appeared in books,
gardened
into the entrance:

the moon crosses over
two sides of the same
star,
how we do know
each other,
the destination
in question,

here is how we fall—
shortly,
pleasantly.

WHAT ARE YOU DOING IN THE RIVER, WHICH HERE, HUMBLY,
isn't golden tonight, but maybe tomorrow will swallow whole
the passersby a little bit in love. We'll go together.

What messages do you receive from those waves: But now
the colours of water where we think this leaves us
are not so different. You are still breathing.

What was that wind, chosen to take care and name it, hiding,
while not mentioning the good news we've been waiting for.
Since that day I go on loving you and am small.

And if I could write a poem for women have changed.
And if I could write a poem for women are still interesting.
And if I could write a poem only for the river.

A WEEK OF KINDNESS ENDS with kisses thrown at her feet my arms expressing the lead-lined sorrow as if somehow removed from the accidental.

The note read the next time it rains come see me but preserve stars and bring us the morning or try.

And don't because of another language skin on sand lily-of-the-valley.

And make me as Claude Cahun was where is she now in her home on the island of Jersey or Paris or Jersey.

I can still hear her voice on the stairs.

For now another language will not fight any further than to say how I can't at the moment seem to reach her.

From here the rest and the danger of rest.

Where this leaves us chosen to see if I was yesterday to the listened.

Her contempt for a body message and a quiet life only tomorrow the note read the night stars might once more uncurl over the river not far from your house.

Here too our most selfish behaviour can be beautiful.

Her crown over grey hair over the river surrendering to the last of hurtful summer.

O to sit in silence for hours with ginger and marigold radiating the river alive while Claude Cahun autumns.

And when will peace violently settle on this gentle hill I know it's late but am leaving the binding of this to her.

Only tell me if the river is too far.

Against the equator against the sun maybe some good news tomorrow and movement.

In September like that sentiment was over her voice in another language not a note not accidental but how easy it is to unmask the stars.

Or it's the difference between appeal and expression.

This closed eyelid on teeth breathing I will never be finished leave my mind is made up is the river at night.

But perhaps Claude Cahun herself is only a womb and for me this was too much.

Though it is not because of the river.

Does she think it's good or bad that some unseen god has pushed us here and there is a heart extenuating in another language.

A heart lifted in surrendering to kisses.

A small body falling by the riverside and in the flow our voices again the colour of water.

A note amid leaves in silt the line make me as Claude Cahun was working.

It's late I know it's late.

It's the final line not a hard letter for secrets or long losses.

Claude! The angel is a dark market! We are transfixed!

> I upset myself dangerously for those I love. Warning: you are among those.
> —Claude Cahun

Steven Jones 1971-1996

THIS CITY BRIDGE TODAY IS CALLING FOR YOUNG MEN,
so growing it becomes only beauty now, and
below, the trees do not die when one thinks they should;
some sort of hope in their suffering branches or
perhaps living beside the valley for too long
has left me a little morbid. Also the cold
finally appeared and with it an acquaintance
of ice slivers spreading over the storm windows.

My cousin fell here in June—along with many
before and after, the line of jumpers not held
fast by consideration for fairer seasons—
though even now it's hard to tell where the bridge ends
and Bloor Street begins, grinding as it does like a
swarm of bees into the city centre. Those bees
are a little quieter this winter, at least,
but, what, inspired by an influx of ladybugs?

Jena saw one today and it's January,
the weather having kept us confused for so long
that insects too are lost in families of sun
and snow, while here as elsewhere, the clouds pour over
street and cars, buses, subways, new traffic tickets, old
pedestrians, commercial billboards and then me.
Still it's a nice change without the sun sometimes as
the water below doesn't really need lighting.

That June I was not thinking of the sunlight on
Aegean ports, the nakedness of bodies and
bodies, the raft to catch him from—only the air
into which he fell, his risk. And that risk taken
before the open stretch of river, stepping on
treetops and disturbing birds and butterflies then,

the orange of their late-night nesting unfluttered
by his sudden appearance in their sleeping midst.

And with that risk passed over—no explanation
necessary, though there's a note I've never seen—
the bed undone, his life no longer restricted,
the moment came when listening for the call of
this city bridge and all he'll never know seemed right.
I would follow him there, but what was he thinking?
Wondering will I be asleep, or else driving,
these ideas together in my indifference.

ALONG THE SHORE OF THE WINTER-COLOURED RIVER:
all who succumb to amorous promise; a dog-scared
skunk chasing Paul Querengesser; my right hand
and my other; those throwing love without weight;
anyone upset with Matthew Yeldon; the winner who
didn't finish the race; my grandmothers; the voice not
of original sin but of original difference; Gillian Best
awake and unfolded; a raccoon reflecting on place;
hand-on-knee Jena Schmitt; swallows in brown clover;
the Queen of Georgia of course; Sue Sinclair the enemy
of stemware; nieces and nephews; anxious mallards;
Laura Manni blushing at the cold of today; my sister
and her sister; all who succumb to amorous despair;
bandy-armed Martin Byrne and his bouncing baby
girls; my mother without gallstones; my father without
glue on his shirt; those not believing love can be
thrown weightless; Gary and Nadia Edmonds driving
under a crescent moon; free mouths upon mouths;
Vicky Chainey-Gagnon in some other realm; the
birthday boys and girls; every bird which cannot
sing a new song; that is you Ilana Luther; not one
casual lover; what is in me that sees in you; yes, Aubie
Golombek. Singly and altogether. None of us cold or tired.

And above the wrought and woven bridge:
sailors upon the sea, rangers throughout the forest,
shepherds over the hill, miners under the mountain,
farmers about the field and in the valley poets.

for —

ANYWAY THAT HOUR FOR REMEMBERING HAS PASSED.
Books worth keeping are back on shelves—any
embarrassment soon forgotten—and that same hour
when you were awake and naked against my equally
naked arms and mouth divides into days over which
your own youth will end. Tell me anyway that eucalyptus
burdens daffodils blooming in the window. Tell me
the sea isn't blue but green. Tell me the days do go
slowly but it's not unnatural that way. Anyway.
Anyway that hour for remembering has passed.

Other books are stored and might not surface again.
Along with them any dream of an ocean knowing full
well that the street and doorway where we hid from
teeth tearing at our bellies and fell but never collapsed
is another ocean. Pilgrim I dreamed last night of a
vessel on this ocean. Pilgrim I dreamed last night of
finding Saint Christopher in a good friend's home.
Pilgrim I dreamed last night of those books which
will never be read for any other nakednesses.
Other books are stored and might not surface again.

There before the window a pale body exposed.
Among what I thought were daffodils and kalanchoe
are the dark inks of your flesh sad friend and the
change in holding a city between your lover's
knees. Well who can see this change? Who can
carry the nudity of a body around forever in this
day and age? Who can die of jealousy or flounder
in the ocean or dare consider a once lost avenue
the point of departure for a final liaison? Well?
There before the window a pale body exposed.

CALL IN THE YOUNG MEN
call them working before burdened
call in five minutes

I turned from what kept you awake
slipped past birds and animals
was unfinished in your frame

Two eyes the length of the sun
in a statute of seventeen months
devouring the pardoned winter

What is unsaid rightly is unkind
when I say exposure to myself
meaning the passage in its sleep

While the empty hours of sickness
watch me working and burdened
call me with the young men

"HOW WILL THIS BE DIFFERENT?" SAID POET TO PROSER,
"The newly blind follow at double arm's length,
Elsewhere accepting an ancestor's fetish
Are letters of loss read for long-lasting strength."

"O does that valley," said coward to champion,
"Seem scumbled and broken in your dreams too,
The river's fidelity fallen in stature,
The waves' disappointment departed anew?"

"Have I misunderstood," said server to subject,
"In trying to sweeten these thoughts with your grace?
Will success come with writing a simpler verse,
Are last words not the same describing this place?"

"It won't my dear"—said proser to poet
"I'm better now"—said champion to coward
"You're on to me"—said subject to server
That day we discard the days we discard.

The Spine of Cities (1935)

For André Breton

with Anastasia Koros, from the Greek of Andréas Embiricos

Spring as Always

I covered the waves of the conquered village with her red dress
First small and then large
Climbed to the castle's tower
And took hold of the clouds and crushed them against her breasts
There was never a deeper wound than hers
There was never a more burnt look in one person's face
There was never in our understanding a longer offering
An offering of confession more varied more full than the clouds tell of
Here and there guillotines are cutting
Warm drops fall on the earth
A mound of earth forms at the most precise point
To this day it is filling and climbing
No curfew is heavier than these drops
No diamond heavier
No lover more full of passion
The mound's smooth black lips shine in the sunlight
At the summit a basin
Full to the top
From its waters a tiny divine girl rises
Hope for our tomorrow.

The Barrier

for Nikitas Randos

Past the crevice past the granite works
The cliff is sending its howl
Flowers from winter have stopped breathing
Velvet drops fall in front of a mirror
The fund has drained itself
An old woman stands on the sand noticing the sea's age
So that her face is hollowed by wind
And her white hair wraps itself around a ship's mast
Her bones becoming stripped of flesh
All the while she kneads her fingers
A spanish woman dancing a tango
Inebriated by the fantasy of Grenada
Is watched by grenadians
While their cells transform themselves
A bee emerges and is lost in the wind
A rose blossoms in its spot
The dancer's castanets are taken by the wind
And it begins to whistle like a crocodile once whistled
But the beach's drama doesn't exist here
Only the ambassador of Grenada exists
And he stands at the dock's edge
Awaiting the arrival of his beloved.

The Flesh of the Olive

Above the meeting of waters contaminated by a sickness forever curing
The steam of health rises and pleases
Belief in the adventure has not lessened
Her eyes are green and reflect in the waters of youth
There a young man meets a young woman and kisses her
Intoxicating words pouring from their lips
And all of their life resembles a meadow
Villas here and there decorating the grassland
Youth youth how well-kept your hair is
Your charms decorated by almond flowers blossoming in a distant valley
The triumphant caesars pass through this place sometimes and lead the gardens' waters away
The women of the gardens plead with them uncovering their breasts
A strand of pearls drips into a funnel
Each pearl is one droplet and each droplet a baby boy
His fortress was demolished and now children play in the shadows
And the lady in the tower's mirror has shattered and the shards are pebbles
Thrown by young warriors in their rock war.

The Friendship

When the feathery down of the day touches the bird
The dust falls and in its place the naked animal jumps
The men don't waste the early hours and begin to work
Screaming tomorrow tomorrow quickly turning their desire
Towards warm breasts that have never forgotten the cool wind
Or caresses brought on by both roundness and intense feelings
In this way tomorrow becomes today
And all at once the walls of the villa fall
Veils are dropped and lovemaking is exposed
The innermost desire
While in the middle of the square
Groups of people are gesturing quietly
Squeezing their gloves in their hands.

Orion

for Odysseas Elytis

The unplanned season with its storks
Floated by on icebergs travelling westward
In the sun naked crystals naked swallows
And as they descend singing the crossing
Bursting of the earth
Quivers of spring
These ices never lack a path without some type of hope
Each voice's warmth contains its entire meaning
A manner of rushing out
With the hardy storks descending
The sounds of the poles are reborn in the clouds
And nets are pulling fish from yesterday's shadows
The heavens are blissful and insects fly about
This gift is an illusion
It's not necessary for seagulls to hide
The sailors standing look for the horizon
An ark appears on Ararat
And a nereid is drawn by an olive branch
Her teeth holding a ring
Her fingers have freedom of speech
Her message comes from afar
We waited thirty years on the icebergs crossing with the siren
When we heard the boat whistling
And the siren appeared smiling
She waited wholeheartedly for us from the morning
For when words are hurried voices reach
And storks fly above us in her light
Sunrise sunrise
The sun's way at dawn
The iceberg's descending
The head of each person fills us with red feathers

Many of us smoke pipes of tobacco
Others cigarettes the foam of the sea
And our clamorous approach
Reminds us of a very old city's name
We all run to see if it has appeared
Since the horizon shines
Since it looks like her so much.

Porphyritic Moment

None of the world's tears grow without desire
On the garden fence birds spread their wings
The nearby river brings them closer
The eagle's desire for the white dove
Is a snow-capped mountain peak
When the ice melts we sing in the valleys
The waters having made us drunk
And our pupils wash these treasures
Some blonde and some dark
In their face they have our hope's reflection
On their breasts the milk of our life
And we stand around them
Eternal orders surrounding us all
The clots of the mountain beating quickly and dissolving
Their snows are songs of the coming year
These years are our life
In hollowed-out trees birds take their afternoon rest
None of the world's tears grow without desire to grow
From time to time we become clepsydras
Sponges struggling for our every drop.

In View of the Morning Hours

for Yves Tanguy

The natural energy
Transmits the dove's pulse
Tears of the river falling constantly
They are tears of joy that can't be covered
They are rivers of old never living never sun-bleached storks
No southwest wind nests in sugarcane
And if at times a shot falls then the clouds lift
And rise separated in layers
There where the corvettes lower their sails
Back on earth a shadow is searching for her lost body
Stolen by the climates of the valley
The fog which hides it thickens
The lake's treasures worry and shiver
The seaweed and the most important life tremble in the depths
One jellyfish cries for yesterday when the lake was transparent
That will return with the first firework
Before winter weather
Before anyone even thinks to light the lamp
Under which one very blonde woman is thinking about her future
The lighthouse-keeper bends towards her lips and kisses them
Like the kiss of walls closing in the seafarers.

Nostalgia and, Also, Anomie

...And right away she then
leaned against his shoulder, shutting her eyes
against a deep, mild light...

—Yannis Ritsos

The words won't change again. Sad friend, you cannot change.

—Elizabeth Bishop

"My Home Is Huge"

First by the door a couch remaindered by
previous tenants. But let us move on.
This wood table, focus for the room, was
once CNIB property but now
supports paper and bamboo, a crystal
ball and tealights as well as it once did
the blind. As a young poet has kissed three
women on the floral couch, under the
south-facing window, I'll not hear a word
against its value. This strapped chair is fine
but the salmon one over beside the
radiator represents, well, with a
blanket wrapped around your knees little else
need be added and the view in summer
of neighbourhood backyards full of trees and
kids wondering where days go in the old
afternoon sun—if I'm to be somewhere
then where? No, no table for your writing here.
Art prints, yes, and potted plants, everything
has a story. Let's move on. The kitchen.
Only two elements of four work on
the stove and the fridge leaks water like no
tomorrow. Table seats three, microwave
is pre-digital. The hanging bronze plate
says handmade in Greece 800 B.C.,
at this time unverified. We're west of
the door now, and the bathroom is blue.
Let's move on. The bedroom has two closets,
one smaller, and drawers built into the wall
for linen. A bookshelf full of dirty
French novels and thin poetry facing
the bed on the north wall, three pillows and

a few blankets—it's been cold what with one
of the storm windows gone. The desk is yours.
Push the computer aside if need be.
You know all these poor things can go elsewhere.

One's Silence as Watchword for Wealth

Let us be fair to the Museum of
Civilization. Let us be fair to
its clockwork employees of times past. Let
us be fair to the underside of its
belly, its rotten teeth, its distance from
us now.
           I have you, monolith, in my
head today, dear old Douglas Cardinal's
curves around your pavilions of rocks
and arrowheads. And I'm giving you up.
I'm giving up for, you see, modern and
beautiful though you are something's not right.
The forearm closes over the elbow
with you; the elbow over the bicep;
the bicep over the shoulder—all that's
in between one and the other.
                            What's new?
The clock ticking past our attraction to
the sanatorium; tools of basic
communication that don't work; water
smelling of crude and alkaline. Too much.
Bear your plight, be fair, within a vale of
tears if you must, but keep me out of it.

Of a City After the Broken-Backed Hero Has Departed

When the city founders first began planning, it was decided that no feature, no landmark or building, the city over, should be more majestic than the hero, whom they knew would arrive in time to defeat an invading army, slay a lion, marry the king's daughter, etc. And so industry, theme parks and airports were built by the waterfront; a highway in the valley; an infinite tower near the palace. Foreign poets were invited to mythologize the hero's presence; they stayed and made homes. Everyone was expecting the hero to arrive, but no one planned for him to leave. After the tragedy, drama unfolds on a poem in the shape of a city. For the poets are left with only two choices: To write of before or to write of after—it having become a cliché to write of during. But whether prophesying or lamenting, the poets' memory has forgotten that the city itself was never majestic. And so verse is written praising the strength of industry; the theme parks in summer; the airport's architecture; the drive through the valley; the tower's symbolism. The founders, confused by whether their initial mistake was planning for the hero's arrival or not planning what to do with the poets after his departure, find themselves able neither to abandon the city nor to assist its recovery. While growth continues, citizens—working in factories, overseeing rollercoasters, maintaining roads—must live within the double nature created by the poets. Each day work is done while thinking of a brighter future; at night, over dinner, toasts are made to better days gone by.

The Illustrious House of Insomnia

At night arrows fell upon her like love.
The good and bad of such a memory:
Delight in broken hearts; a kind of shove
against the body; the mind's reverie
at night; arrows falling on her like love.

Then, in the experience of darkness,
arranging furnishings of her future
home and life along with some sleepless
and wearying need of hers to endure
then, in the experience of darkness,

O Greece! she smiled, O Rome! The old world!
I am, sooner or later, thinking of
ways to return you, prefigured and pearled,
to a today where one decides on love,
O Greece, smiling, O Rome! The old world!

Her vigilance is, of course, narrow, too
nocturnal to aid dramas unfolded
over dinner or drinks, fully set-to
with severity but through the eyelid
her vigilance is off course, narrow, too.

And if this is only the beginning,
restfulness coming over her like waves,
a ship at sea with a captain shouting,
Down below, mateys! Our watery graves
await! This is only the beginning!

then tonight might pass more quickly for her—
accordingly in cotton panties, nightshirt,
barefeet and loose bottoms, a reporter
details daydreams, a diurnal expert
helping the night pass more quickly for her

as though the day never ended at dusk.
Except that what went wrong did. This sudden
longing for her everyday in dreams, brusque
words for the little lost tragedienne
who felt her day didn't just end at dusk.

But seeing is believing and living
through a thought that began at bedtime and
finished before breakfast is her ending.
Please for one night let her, in this way, stand
against seeing, believing and living.

This evening please let her find thumbed shut
beside her the eyelids of more than some
childhood remnant, once loved and now corrupt.
Let her disengage herself and succumb
this evening, please, let the moon thumb shut

her eyes to passing towns and villages
on a journey with no destination
other than a night's sleep not in pages
of some book or her imagination:
Let her eyes, closed, pass towns and villages.

The Banker's Wife

Honestly Miss Honey Bee, I'll never forget you.
And while the world may spit you out its eye
in deference to your stance on domestic issues,
your jabbering husband and I...I...I..., what happened
was this—always your gaze fixed on a Picasso-filled
museum case at the Albright-Knox and, as for me,
what happened is this—the call came in and
Balthus is dead, my dear Miss Undershirt, surrender,
the last of the great last-namers has left us for
the front. In the five minutes left of nudity
before the memory of your skin takes over,
O Matisse, every scale and plate is now with me.
And you too Miss Post-War Nationalism.
In the half-light, you looked better than any
primitive painting or perhaps a wingless tyrant
but from that day by the lake there's little left
where there should be something, don't you think,
more than our discussion of Derain or the implications
of Futurism in the 21st Century—like the clouds
in the sky or birds in the trees, Miss Tempest Passing.
I'd call to hear your eyes light up but when he answered
there would be rest and room to sit at least, here,
my ear to his senseless breathing as yours is,
only really, at our age, Miss Detail of Still Life.

Artist and His Muse

for Aubie Golombek

I would speak to you not as lover this morning
but as the wounded lens through which Longinus
drove his spear some years ago, as great a thing
as to be living when an age passes. Something of the
suffering too, waking here to find these berries under
her beautiful lips, red and wondrous among
the wondrous things pulled from earth in spring,
at a time when our fingers fill with topsoil and the
roots of young trees, graves then, but also beginnings.

The ripeness of the flesh can sicken, inflict upon
the bearer fevers and neural disorders, but so does
pollen leave some sniffling, or the dander of
household pets. This could be what you have gathered.
Like so many leaves, borrowed if you love them,
the hours fall on us and glass, light breaking through
each shard, no, not light, but what the heart gathers,
longing, springing inward and outward.
                                        Last night
it wasn't Aristotle who awoke and coveted the arms
and breasts of woman but there is a remnant of his
tongue on the sheets. And her breasts were born to
this moment, much of it expected by their reserve,
but theirs is only one thing among the many and that
lightning another and that rise. Charge. Expectation
is our enemy and the knowledge that we may not love
always and anyone but do look forward to the moment.

Summer has come suddenly this year. Not much to show
for it here, as usual, except a collection of plastic bags
and an unread selection of books. There are, too, the
marks of her body to contend with. Once scraped into the
mattress where we lay and now in this poem, effortlessly
and boundlessly as it seems, the past has cradled us,
bearing some attraction but also the shine of the new,
more modern, more perfect than we had seen.
                                                       Or this is
what we understood when we loved and began to think
like human beings and making things our own. When
memory and regret seemed beautiful and the time
was right for us to collect ideas into something formal
and her breasts and body fit there, moulded with our
intentions if only for a moment. But then that moment
is what we're made of and something else for which
we're never to be forgiven. In any case, light, or its
absence, is your jurisdiction. And the only sorrow will
come out of love for the unobtainable, its tragic fulfillment
flawed by the opening of our eyes.

Nationalism Is the Vice of Our Age

I am writing this with my back to the fence,
at the foot of a great oak in the avenue near
your apartment. It is the second Sunday in July
and the best part is not sinking through the earth
at night but flying over rooftops counting the
new branches from spring to fall. After two-thousand
years, to be here, covered over in all of five seconds
by a youth running naked in the parking lot, Eros.
Here the mess made by mankind of nature. And, with
worries and restraint, a telling of more than
experience can teach, all the greens of summer
and families of mint surrounding roots, soil, moss,
a latticed fence, at once both clear and fervent,
the tools dressed, undressed, and redressed. But all
this intuition is too much for some. Where
the moss grows insects follow and there's weeding
to be done. It's going to rain. There are many
sacrifices to be made before working and there are
those here who still can work without seducing each
other or selling a way of life and are in love and
wonderfully sexual in their own way. One need not
believe, What a life I am leading! when mornings
in July are the finest mornings and end only with
thoughts of a well-ordered age previous to our own.
In a short, sweet time, quiet Eros, wet to the bone with
rainwater, will again make meadows, grass, bees,
dandelions, saplings and violets accessible and as
noble as lovers lying snug and warm in bed,
protected from the damp, cool night by their long
memories and fear of being alone. At this very
moment, however, beside an anthill formed at the foot
of an oak whose inhabitants prepare for the

coming storm, I suddenly remember, years ago,
drawing into myself away from a vast stretch of
country and towards the miniature scale of the ant's
world, the sensual greed of their daily work and
understanding amid the tar and concrete of this lot.
The first call of thunder at 11:45 p.m., this may take
all night, may take a held moment away. There's
an opening in your apartment where the wind
rushes through, not a window but a river by way
of a wall. Flying back tonight, I will pass, unhindered,
a breeze unto your dank skin, the pilled blue sheets
no defense against the coming weather.

The Wild Bride

How like you to found a city
in your summer wedding dress. Or
better still the night outside, a cool breeze
through the window and there a house
lit up and there a garage open and
there a single star. I'm feeling better
about this already—trees rustling now—
perhaps a car drives past with you in it
and not long after a young woman
laughs in the street. I think for the
time being, though, that some focus should be
given to the calendar of events following
tonight's entertainment, the growing need to
wake from a sleep as light as the moon
or conceivably a sparrow. I'm holding you
to this now that the garage has closed and
the house gone dark. Look how the clouds
fold and disappear, covering everything but
that one, dim star. If I made my wish on it,
played out superstition to tonight's conclusion,
would everything work out, be believable,
has this only been one night and there
you are, still in your wedding dress,
waiting for the sun to rise and it's late.

Harold Town's *In Air Above the Poet's House* (1956)

Let's just say that this went unspoken for a few years
and then suddenly occurred to Georges Braque in 1912.

Let's just say that if you look for once above my house
you might see these things, sure, but to whose benefit?

Let's just say that the air moves here, the dishes aren't done,
that if one locks the door something is definitely left out.

Let's just say that it's easy to spot the colours and shapes, but
what's more difficult is pointing out the fair-skinned woman.

Let's just say our eyes focus readily on flatness, spellbound
by Greenberg's theories of texture and expression.

Let's just say our version is less muddy, less chaotic than
the New York school, more accessible than Washington's.

In fact, let's even go as far as to be ingracious for sights
that critics point out, leaving our thoughts to the heavens.

In fact, let's imagine how we might be airplanes tonight
and could fly this area comfortably without ever landing.

For we can appreciate colour and light without a word of
assistance from poets and as if a painter declared only this.

For we are open-minded enough to mingle with the two ideas,
distinctly, and distinguish the inconspicuous from the bare.

Open Guidebook

Some say I love you, that it's not too late.
That when the film ended and we mocked the
guest-speakers and threw popcorn there was a
doorprize for someone long dead who couldn't
win. Did you know that already? It was
the first time the sight of a woman's breasts left
me numb. And then followed your stupidest
instructions yet: Open this book, read like
a man who has spent his entire life
in pursuit of love, cherished, but also

now ashamed for—No, I thought, not now with
your disappearing act so near. It's late.
Anyway, the book already seemed to
know all this and predicted a career
in commercial television for its
readers: Actors in beer ads and other
so-called literary forms. Well, I read
it on my own time, then and there, but not
before letting you know how I felt in
regards to the content laid out for me:

AMSTERDAM

When I say I will not return, meaning it literally, I mean a yellow restaurant in this city with one table for two and six people where each set shares a turn waiting for a table, eating at a table and waiting on a table.

ATHENS

The sun first, opening on the streets like a—I want to say bullet—poem by Elytis. Two men in suits passed below our window, larger and sharper than candles but half as sad.

BARCELONA
The bees here don't work weekends. Lying beside the ocean, two young girls play-fighting in the sand, and around us not only the waters but also the knowledge that we will never meet again.

BILBAO
Can't write any poems in the Casco Viejo, only sentences that don't connect. I close my eyes and see myself being kissed, being lunged at, eager.

BOSTON
And there we had and raised our family, the silence, and the endless preservation of thank yous, like that, year in and out.

BUFFALO
What you think of as unsuspecting customs officers are really the grander-than-all types who run this town. But have you seen the museum? It keeps a certain kind of tourist coming back.

BUFFALO
I split my finger—there they are—the children and their children and the absence of last night, lost like the street lamp on the hill.

CHATHAM
The Japanese woman in the shoe store said it was good luck to have toes like yours, so I threw out the rabbit's foot, the horseshoe, and took down the quarter taped above the door. I knew now where to find luck.

DELPHI
I dreamed of an older oracle where Marcel Detienne, explaining function in discontinuous syllables, appeared to have become an orange rind amid marble and broken columns.

DETROIT
I want to finish this tonight but conceivably, no, the motor city at midnight seen from the back of a midsize sedan is not the moment of worship you mentioned.

DODONI
Could an oracle predict an oracle? And why would/wouldn't it? Only an olive tree growing out of the rubble could know the answer simply, like listening to you walk around your apartment from where I sleep.

ETOBICOKE
Please, this evening, won't you?

HOLLYWOOD
Spring night in rain. Wind whipping bugs against green mesh and snapping palm leaves in a story by an old woman whose husband's death has left her castrated.

KASTORIA
This city must be blind for the mosquitos here are maybe the largest for miles around and to tell the truth one can stop scratching the bites without ever quite finishing.

LONDON
The setting sun and now, gone out to see the world, Tiresias whispers, "Every day I need fewer and fewer people." It's as simple as that.

LOS ANGELES
Lips. Lights in the horizon form enclaves in the desert. And what do you suppose that strip of lights is? Collapsed behind the door, a pile of skin and hair, the bones gone.

MADRID
There are too many lovers in Spain, anxious to show they are loving and being loved.

MIAMI
How could we never know the future here? But we were listening and did know. The star that fell that evening? Every now and then the neighbourhood lights shone through it.

MONTREAL
Gypsum or alabaster, maybe it's better that all I want to see is your underwear. If it's all you can give. And if you tell me in the morning.

MUSKOKA
These days are all about water.

MYKONOS
These days are all about waste.

NEW YORK CITY
Propylaea.

NIAGARA FALLS
Ah, we never did talk about love. Perhaps separate beds are in order or else, the moment of mystery having passed, let us find life outside this living.

ORLANDO
You have stopped speaking to me or there is nothing to say or we have never spoken or I will tell you in Montreal tomorrow morning following the local weather forecast.

OTTAWA
Line found in a letter left between pages of a copy of Julio Cortázar's *Hopscotch* in the National Library from actress Selma Blair to an imaginary lover up past his bedtime: Isn't it the body you want?

PAMPLONA
The Roman road through the city walls. Hunger. She and I sat in the shade of a tree by the ruins and finished a lunch of egg sandwiches and cold beer.

PARIS
How many ways are there to write what one will never stop learning? A dozen? Today I saw footage of a young man telling a crowd of onlookers, *"Je suis un poète. Vraiment. C'est que mes pied dans l'eau actuellement."*

QUEBEC CITY
J'ai tout regard.

ROCHESTER
Is that John Ashbery's birthplace or the House of Guitars on the chopping block? Don't answer until you develop control over your sentence fragments.

ROME
Wanted: Virgin Mary soap dispenser, MTV Europe, Superman, Sistine Chapel ceiling, pantheon, Paul McCartney and Wings, apologia, local disco, busride to Pompeii, beer at McDonald's. All these things and then and there, perhaps, a first girl to fall in love with.

THESSALONIKI
The old Turkish walls, the tower by the sea, Marianthe. Ah. Something is lost in the symbolism, surely. When one sets goals low, it happens all the time.

TORONTO
What would you like me to say? You make me delirious.

VANCOUVER
It's like this. Everyone here seems to adore Simon Armitage. I mean, really, am I the only one holding back even a little?

VICTORIA
Sunset, skyline, clouds, cliffs, bushes, ashes, concrete, metal, beach, logs, detritus, seaweed, so long.

WESTON
Detail: Founded 1796 on the banks of the Humber.

Song for —, Leaving

Not June that year but the summer of a love
where a woman, singing, could be heard and with
some luck understood by those around her.

And still that same fear pours out under the
stars of Orion: A constellation less changed over the
centuries than the quiet of the countryside.

Her song of scorpion and hunter betrays the reeds
calling Orpheus! Orpheus! in the peaceful wind,
now rising, suddenly, vividly, in one who is absent.

Silent poplars and birch trees hanging under the moon
of men who have lost their accoutrements to the heavens
in music or desire, the two made one at least here.

By the lake mosquitoes and near the house wind
coming up on its own to gather her singing into
the sharpness of a man's drunken challenge to the gods.

O hang her in the stars, too, Calliope, prepare a feast
with wine and black olives, cheese and cold chicken,
the freshest wildflowers growing over the table.

And on her face the touch of water and his starry fingers
and a little farther on the silence of the forest where
she is the one absent and the song not hers alone.

A Good Life

Little fisher of men. No new movements today.
Like a man learning guitar under a yellow birch.
Air through the open window smelling of his music.
And since hearing it the lovers downstairs have woken.
Lately it seems that any little thing excites them.
But does a man learning guitar please anyone but himself?
Possibly. The birch still grows. And they go on below.
And on. She came—you can imagine—I hear it all.
Is this my memory—maybe it's going. And how to decide?
I know the life I'm leading now is a good one.
Such a natural thing to hear. His fingers on the fretboard.
Her voice in the air. Good morning I thought.
Or good night. Though the difference meant little.
How it can be light and dark outside at the same time.
Here at the end of a moment. Learning guitar for two lovers.
A strange entertainment for answering a thirst.
And it's the first I knew of that player under the birch.
His simple performance of song. An addition.
He played to me. Not only to me. But to me. Too.

A Poetics of Highways

The great function of poetry is to give us back the situations of our dreams.
—Gaston Bachelard

In our time Apollo is sound asleep.
—Guy Davenport

Inventory

One car four tires three hub caps
One sentence fragment
One man of the world who is no longer the man he was

A postcard of Picasso's *Seated Woman* 1927
Astrud Gilberto singing "Corcovado"
A lactating breast from a poem by Embiricos

The Pocket Oxford Greek Dictionary
The cover page of a daguerreo-essay, first draft, entitled "Beach Boys
    References in the Works of Guy Davenport"
The Water Margin

Samuel Beckett's headstone
Separate beds
Someone to yearn for

Cavafy's death mask on a purple pillow
Circe's botanical sketches, in pastels and water-colour (Richard Outram)
Cybermen attacking a policebox

One sweet memory I can enter
One 4 x 6 photograph of André Breton opening his eyes on the Gaspé
One ginger ale one granola bar in a green package one swiss-cheese
    sandwich with tomato lettuce and mayonnaise

Elizabeth Bishop's eczema
Eduardo Chillida's lines
Eight neglected road-safety measures

Lattimore's *Iliad* and *Odyssey*
L'argent pour payer les fleurs (Jacques Prévert)
Lies never believed

All the lazy bees of Spain
A flower I've loved since childhood (A.F. Moritz)
A three-year run of the *North York Mirror*

The life of Louis Riel—retold by Disney
The serving jug of Ganymede
The trotting animal can restore red hearts to red (Anne Carson)

Thirty kilometres of concrete
Toi d'aujourd'hui que j'aime par-delà moi-même (Paul Eluard)
Thoughts suitable to a sanatorium (W.H. Auden)

Weston Home of the Bicycle
What we can talk about that will take all night
Writing from George Seferis to America during the war

Many many symbolic drawings of fish
Mark Rothko's *Untitled (Violet, Black, Orange, Yellow on White and Red)* 1949
Marble-shoed Tiresias

Her last two hours with another man
Hadjidakis' soundtrack to *Never On Sunday*
Hayao Mayazaki's aeroplane designs

Napoleon's penis
Northrop Frye's temperance
Nestor's counsel

The rediscovery of Monsieur le Pauvre
The plans for my return
The sun as seen setting from the Hotel Arana, Bilbao, Spain, May 28,
    1999

A strip of lights in the desert that is not Las Vegas
A recurrent dream of the dead
A well-chosen door leading outside this house

Brother Album ST-9002
Books by little-known poets
Beatle Ringo's sacrificial ring

Speculation on the relationship between Goethe and Charlotte von
    Stein
Stitches to show something's missing (Sylvia Plath)
Some ungodknown reason

A 27-years-dead painter
A list of names associated with the moon
A videotape showing Mavis Gallant walking slowly on the Rue du Four,
    6^e, Paris

The Welsh word for summer
The Alice B. Toklas Cookbook
The morning of a wedding day

The Example of Insomnia at 100 km/h

My commentary becomes too precise:
The driver who muttered, car flipping over and scraping along thirty
    feet of cement,
"That's it for me. I love you all."
And then survived with minor back pains.
As you might guess, it is easy to forget.
But a clumsy lover is a clumsy lover.

The Example of Amnesia Between Departure and Destination

What I'm really saying this morning is that you wear
the sun like a hillside.
You are bees with dandelions below.
This morning, thank you, but it's you who needs looking after.
This morning for a wedding.
Or the undertaking of extensive road repairs.

The Example of Tailgating

There are moments when I am in love with you.
"For safety," whispers the driver, half-smiling,
"we're going to have our affair done right."
—Grips the wheel tighter, thinking please don't hit me.
And semen on everything.
While the fields outside pass less pleasantly.

The Example of Gathering Dandelions by the Roadside

Work cuts the heart.
And at midday, when hungry and thirsty,
the edible leaves are bitter but not sorrowful.
When will I get back to the house—
a love letter under my pillow.
When will I get back to the heart.

The Example of Driving
Under the Influence

What the driver will say there:
"I am growing older,"—starting his next sentence with,
"I must tell you,"—and then does or doesn't;
each blade of grass bending
and breaking in the fields of lines.
What we will say in those fields of lines.

The Example of Passing on the Right

During the drive home, an argument between
windshield and left side-view mirror:
rain falls forever and again on the gone roads;
deep rain from summer and, oh help me, above all,
help me in evening to see clearly the eddying traffic.
Dear —, nothing fell today but rain.

The Example of Passing on the Left

Once more around those selfsame vehicles,
browning grass to the south and sun, and
the driver has misunderstood the road,
winding and separating as it does all around.
A trick of light on polished glass:
objects in mirror are more intimate than they appear.

The Example of Passenger-side Hysteria

"I'm sorry this day is over.
The doors are locked, it hurts me to think this way.
This way I might have hurt—cut it, I feel sick.
A first summer look at flowers. I am thinking of—
cut. Want to get married tomorrow, I'm sick.
There is no such thing as regret."

The Example of Sideswiping

"When at last I am lying in bed and telling the sun to leave."
The driver, in his timidity, recalls the still-shaking violets,
and those dandelions I told you about.
The damaged fender goes on like this,
every word from its foul mouth a reminder.
"Oh —, my apologies to you."

The Example of Bumper-to-bumper Traffic

This is the use of talking: a fern reduced to ashes,
dissolved in water, and allowed to evaporate forms again a fern.
I just love you. A thousand tail lights hanging over a heart
and once again, later, up under the clouds.
This is the use of talking:
a heart reduced to ashes.

The Example of Getting to the Church On Time

Only the bees can hear those vehicles
crashing through their walls of air. If the driver remains
at today, the difference between a face memorized and a face
    unrecallable
becomes yesterday—a dream of kissing suddenly a burden.
"I wish I could tell you," he responds,
when asked what sorrow bees know.

The Example of an End to Examples

The answer is hard and hard to remember, coming as it does no
longer, not yet, secretly, up in the air, hurry or you'll miss it.
Though these roads were built to connect us, even the concrete
bundles itself; the wind passing never sings.
Yet I list drivers, dandelions, bees, weddings—I did mention semen—
and only once regret.

Dear —, I Am Leaving Weston

This time last year rained upon by caprice,
every dream and now the phone doesn't help,
and I can't walk to meet you at Jane Street.

While the key to my house was pure Magritte,
the door, as everyone knows, closed itself
this time last year—rained upon by caprice.

How to face an awkwardness of defeat,
when what remains becomes only heartfelt,
and I can't walk to meet you at Jane Street.

What was short-lived or imaginary,
I have saved for this work—simply farewell.
This time last year rained upon by caprice,

our last exchange, and plans never to grieve.
Well, your head wasn't in my arms for health,
and I can't walk to meet you at Jane Street.

Perhaps nothing's to be said of relief,
if these lines are not able to dispel
this time last year and the rain from caprice
and I can't walk to meet you at Jane Street.

Poem for a Prospective Lover Concerning Auden as Failure in Eight Parts

Part One

Wednesday and better men and better and better men
Most nights before sleep I begin by imagining your ecstasy
Tonight a man in a brown owl costume furls of feathers and leaves to whose eyes I am again in love with a stranger to whose eyes the words are not found to whose eyes it is summer and it hurts to whose eyes the years are broken to whose eyes I am as fragile as my mother fears to whose eyes you don't seem the same
Saturday and I felt so strange yesterday I thought you might call

Part Two

Monday and the trouble with dreams says Auden of course is that other people's are so boring
Wednesday and dream last night we were walking we did not detour past the construction but faced it head-on and ruined our shoes
A young man passed I said that is my cousin see he died a young man every morning and removing your sweater showed me the caterpillar on your bare arm
Friday and what does it mean to dream of the dead I wondered upon waking but you were nowhere to ask your love of me
Sunday and there is no caterpillar on your arm beyond it is still my night

Part Three

Sunday and better men would have kissed you by now your white knees what is endearing when is already ah I can't hide hand reaching for hand for your eyes in memory being able to say everything

Monday and in 1936 Auden writes to a friend that he is off to Spain
	but O I do hope there are not too many surrealists there
Tender Auden who cried and told Isherwood that he could never find
	anyone to love him that he considered himself a sexual failure who
	hated the French who translated *Orphée and Les Chevaliers de la
	Table Ronde* who thought Gide a dreary immoralist but let
	Baudelaire influence *The Orators* and then suppressed it
I am not mistaken you see
Monday and will nothing ever unite us

Part Four

Tuesday and I called last night but you weren't there didn't leave a
	message
What was I saying I'm sorry tomorrow
Wednesday and near the border of sanity says Auden of *The Orators*
Don't be so single-minded you said well first you said don't be so you
	said I like your hat you said want to drop by ah I can't when you
	invite me when you look at me
I am worried about failure and Thursday more later

Part Five

Saturday and sometimes I get so carried away for instance last night
	after dinner I kept thinking ask if you can kiss her and at break of
	day God's flashlight shone where intuition failed at break of day
	excessive love towards a neighbour at break of day the grace of
	being woken by street repairs
Sunday and to better times to better change purses to better locks to
	better soil to better hurting to better distance

The whole Journal ought to be completely rewritten Auden wrote in
   reply to a reader's letter
Thursday and I wonder over and over is there a chance that and never
   finish

   Part Six

Is it you who keeps leaving toothpicks in my toenails
Monday and I am thinking of you as you looked on Monday thinking
   of you leaving as I leave thinking of you luggage in hand thinking
   of you long after the day is over thinking of you drawing holes in
   your generous back
Sunday and the dead are even further than you
O nobody my heart isn't in it
Wednesday and I fall back on your name worrying about Auden and
   Thursday

   Part Seven

Saturday and is today the day for caterpillars and packed bags owls and
   intuition tooth-picks and fragility you've read it all before in the
   mirror worrying what will be made of all this in the everyday
   except Thursday of eroticism
Are these only wounds to another written out of dream and desire
If *The Orators* is Auden's sinister joke on the reader then let it end
   read of your losses he writes to better men and better men making
   reading a way of locking in or holding out of this house as he left
   them there as he left them there

Part Eight

No you are still there
Wednesday and for remembering that breath can be sweet
Wednesday and within the signature of your body a dream why write
    to you beforehand the horror the epilogue well I begin by
    imagining
Now we didn't fall asleep we didn't own the land we didn't rob any
    restaurants we didn't attempt metaphor we didn't express an
    interest
Wednesday and we are unpressed and finished this day and what ought
    I to do

The Driver's Dictionary

A confessional resource to everyday word usage on the street and highway

answer (an′sər, än′-) *n.* **1.** You are new in my dream. **2.** Nothing is lost but something is recovered: And the poet—he shattered in her hands like glass. – *v.* **1.** It's late. Put away your poems. **2.** *Tu as détruit la fête des mères.* **3.** Ring damn you.

bees (bēz) *n. pl.* **1.** Any of a large number of hymenopterous insects carried by every one of the sun's rays. Then everything starts buzzing. **2.** A pure image or sublimation. – Syn. see DANDELION.

canker (kang′kər) *n.* **1.** *Pathol.* Do not bite your cheek. Do not grind your teeth. Consciousness not only suborned but septic. **2.** O but a naked lap to rest my head on!

car (kär) *n.* **1.** What are you going to do to me? **2.** *Poetic* Back in business. **3.** *U.S. Slang* Whole eastern seaboard: Ah yes, yes. – Syn. *Car, automobile, vehicle* and *jalopy* mean a way to get around town. A *car* is a car is a car. An *automobile* is also a car except when it is an automobile. Neither is a *vehicle* because vehicles can travel on water and in the air. One can imagine Gertrude Stein hurling abuse out the window of a *jalopy*, while Miss Toklas, knee-deep in mud, turns the starter crank.

dandelion (dan′də-līən) *n.* A widespread plant.

different (dif′ər•ənt, dif′rənt) *adj.* **1.** Sit still. **2.** One human question: What could be more *different?* **3.** Too, too cruel world. **4.** The muddied bird is resting on a fence. **5.** He climbed up a pile of books until he was standing on top. He stepped over Eliot and Lawrence and by the time he got to Graves he knew no one would ever stop him again.

driver (drī´vər) *n*. **1.** Another ace able to recognize the time of attack. **2.** *M'aidez! M'aidez!* **3.** A lifelong Lothario.

insomnia (in·som´nē·ə) *n*. The enemy of highways. [<L <*insomnis* sleepless <*in-* without + *somnus* sleep]

intimacy (in´tə·mə·sē) *n*. **1.** A blonde ability. **2.** Pity on others and on ourselves. **3.** The damage caused by this. **4.** Everything you want me to: I do remember the dire *intimacy* of it all.

intimate (in´tə·mit) *adj*. **1.** Uninhibited, generous: I hear your voice when you are not here. **2.** Start by undoing a button. **3.** And the small necks of women: do we forever hold our mouths from or on them? **4.** Something more than the time of day.

lipogram (lip´o·gram) *n*.

, etc. [after Li Po, 700-762, Chinese Poet +<F gramme <LL *gramma* small weight <Gk. gramma]

marriage (mar´ij) *n*. **1.** If your mother is waiting in the car, you *should* go: I think you are doing this on purpose. **2.** Desperation: a last revolt. **3.** Where this revolt is missing, poetry is lost. **4.** Endure but rainy weather.

masturbation (mas´tər·bā´shən) *n*. Loneliness, absence, I'd like to quit the habit: piddle. [<L *mastur·batio, -onis*] – masturbator *n*. – masturbatory *adj*. For an index of masturbators from Portnoy to Ulysses consult and consult.

motorcycle (mō´tər·sī´kel) *n*. Tell me the truth about the death of civilized man so that woman is more than one. Would you ever think of ellipsis. – *v.i.* **·cled, ·cling** You and I have no interest—but the driver, he marvels at such things. [after slurring of *Martin*, name of a British citizen in Canada who mentioned this only while driving + <Gk. *kyklos* circle] – motorcyclist *n*.

personalized (pûr′sən·əl·īzd′) *adj.* **1.** I've been building: trying to express something but can't, repetition: the example of an accompaniment to *personalized* licence plates. **2.** Such strange ways. **3.** We'll make an exchange: you put your head on my chest and I'll kiss you.

rear-impact (rir′im′pakt) *adj. U.S. & Canadian* **1.** Beardless. **2.** Rammed. **3.** Convulsive. **4.** Debutante. **5.** Ulterior. **6.** Undaunted.

rear-view (rir′vyōō′) *adj.* **1.** Pink or tawny behind panties. **2.** Damn the decencies of others. **3.** You have a parka and a dress and some bean bags in a bag by the door. The passé shoes belong to another.

regret (ri·gret′) *v.t.* **·gretted, ·gretting** I'm not asking you to beg. Go inside and lock the door. Pretend you're not there when I come knocking. – *n.* Leave the road forever. Tie one hand in a knot behind your back, and, nightmare after nightmare, well up the loneliness inside your breast, to pour it out of your eyes, so that my heart would break if I didn't stay. [<OF *regreter* < Gmc. Cf. ON *grëta* to weep, OE *grëtan*.]

road-rage (rōd′rāj) *n.* **1.** Please stay tonight. **2.** Different (*which see*). **3.** Different. Intimacy. – road-rageable *adj.* – road-rager *n.*

semen (së′mən) *n.* "What is said is more important than what is not said. What remains to be said is more important than what has been said."

side-view (sīd′ vyōō′) *adj.* **1.** Man is half-open being. **2.** You are on a new road, entering new lanes on the same road. **3.** The grass grows long not tall. **4.** Kill all the witnesses. – *n.* Perfect breasts.

traffic (traf′ik) *n.* How often do we need traffic? This still travels. It's as if you're about to be locked in a triangle: Something wonderful might happen before or after, but in the meantime it will be horrible. How often do we need repetition? – trafficker *n.*

violet (vī ə·lit) *n.* **1.** And then suddenly it was there: the sun partner I gave you. **2.** These love affairs with their everlasting fidelity; especially the common *garden fidelity* (*V. odorata*), and the wild *blue* or *meadow fidelity.* **3.** Duly noted: the turmoil of *violet* passions no longer disturbs the delicious sensations that works of art give. **4.** We so much admire a perfection that is the food of experience. **5.** Food for a mean winter.

wedding (wed´ing) *n.* **1.** Pouring perfume in your hair while you read in bed. **2.** You are eyeteeth and all molars I. **3.** Promise never to do anything like this again.

Index of Titles

Meditation on a Desired Reader 11
The Ivory Gate 14
The Horn Gate 15
Nausicaa 16
Eros 17
Anteros 18
Hesione 19
Lethe 20
Mnemosyne 21
Marsyas 22
Babys 23
Selene 24
Evadne 25
Io 26
Theoclymenus 27
Eos 28
Alcyone 29
Telephones in the Oneiropoems 30

Pardon 33
Tonight at least, wait for me if you possibly can 34
When you were hungry for bread I spoke of bees in the valley 35
Do you grow the night so that we go down further 36
The bridge today was closed 37
What are you doing in the river, which here, humbly 38
A week of kindness ends 39
This city bridge today is calling for young men 41
Along the shore of the winter-coloured river 43
Anyway that hour for remembering has passed 44
Call in the young men 45
"How will this be different," said poet to proser 46

Spring as Always 49
The Barrier 50

The Flesh of the Olive	.51
The Friendship	.52
Orion	.53
Porphyritic Moment	.55
In View of the Morning Hours	.56
"My Home Is Huge"	.59
One's Silence as Watchword for Wealth	.61
Of a City After the Broken-Backed Hero Has Departed	.62
The Illustrious House of Insomnia	.63
The Banker's Wife	.65
Artist and His Muse	.66
Nationalism Is the Vice of Our Age	.68
The Wild Bride	.70
Harold Town's *In Air Above the Poet's House* (1956)	.71
Open Guidebook	.72
Song for —, Leaving	.78
A Good Life	.79
Inventory	.83
The Example of Insomnia at 100 km/h	.86
The Example of Amnesia Between Departure and Destination	.86
The Example of Tailgating	.87
The Example of Gathering Dandelions by the Roadside	.87
The Example of Driving Under the Influence	.88
The Example of Passing on the Right	.88
The Example of Passing on the Left	.89
The Example of Passenger-side Hysteria	.89
The Example of Sideswiping	.90
The Example of Bumper-to-bumper Traffic	.90
The Example of Getting to the Church On Time	.91
The Example of an End to Examples	.91
Dear —, I Am Leaving Weston	.92
Poem for a Prospective Lover Concerning Auden as Failure in Eight Parts	.93
The Driver's Dictionary	.97

Acknowledgements

Thanks to the editors of the following in which some of the poems in this book first appeared:
DESCANT: "The Ivory Gate," "Nausicaa," "Anteros," "Mnemosyne"
THE MALAHAT REVIEW: "The Horn Gate," "Babys,", "Io," "Eos"
POETRY GREECE: "Tonight at least, wait for me if you possibly can,"
    "Anyway, that hour for remembering has passed"
QUEEN STREET QUARTERLY: "Spring as Always," "The Friendship"

"The Driver's Dictionary" appeared, in a slightly different form, in the chapbook DRIVERS, ABSENCE, SNOW (Swashbuckle Books, 2001). "A week of kindness ends" appeared in the chapbook UNSAID POEMS (Swashbuckle Books, 2002); Claude Cahun's post-epigraph is translated by Mary Ann Caws from *The Surrealist Look* (MIT Press, 1999).

The epigraph for ONEIROPOEMS is translated by Richmond Lattimore, from *The Odyssey of Homer* (Harper Perennial, 1991), Book XIX, 560-67. The first epigraph for ON COWARDICE is translated by Kay Boyle, from Crevel's *Babylon* (Sun & Moon Press, 1996); the second is translated by Czeslaw Milosz and Robert Hass, from Milosz's *The Collected Poems 1931-1987* (The Ecco Press, 1988). The first epigraph for NOSTALGIA AND, ALSO, ANOMIE is translated by Edmund Keeley, from Ritsos' *Repetitions, Testimonies, Parentheses* (Princeton University Press, 1991). The second is from Elizabeth Bishop's *The Complete Poems: 1927-1979* (FSG, 1999). The first epigraph for A POETICS OF HIGHWAYS is translated by Maria Jolas, from Bachelard's *The Poetics of Space* (Beacon Press, 1994); the second is from Davenport's *The Jules Verne Steam Balloon* (Johns Hopkins, 1993).

The Greek texts of Embiricos' poems appeared in Ενδοχώρα [Hinterland] (Pleias, 1974).

"Pardon" contains an allusion to Selena Tandon's "in mumbai." The title for "Artist and His Muse" is a mistranslation of Balthus' painting "Le peintre et son modèle," 1981.

Some work on this book took place during the completion of my Master's Degree in Interdisciplinary Studies at York University. I am grateful for the support offered by the department and the university, both intellectually and financially.

Gratitude for assistance in revising this book is owed to Al Moritz, Richard Teleky, Jena Schmitt, Matt Yeldon, Sue Sinclair, Anastasia Koros. My thanks also to Richard Dionne, editor, who supported the book through all stages.